STEP·BY·STEP

CHINESE
Cooking

The Family Circle Promise of Success

Welcome to the world of Confident Cooking, created for you in the
Family Circle® Test Kitchen, where recipes are double-tested by our team
of home economists to achieve a high standard of success.

MURDOCH BOOKS®

Sydney • London • Vancouver • New York

SOUPS & STARTERS

A soup can be served during the meal or at the beginning if preferred. A variety of little dishes or snacks are usually served as an entrée. In this chapter we give you some traditional Chinese favourites.

Spring Rolls

Ideal with drinks.

Preparation time:
  35 minutes
Cooking time:
  12 minutes
Makes about 24

---

1 packet large spring roll wrappers
2 dried Chinese black mushrooms, soaked
120 g skinless chicken breast
2 tablespoons vegetable oil
2 spring onions, finely chopped

100 g bamboo shoots, chopped
½ red capsicum, chopped
120 g bean sprouts, chopped
1 tablespoon dark soy sauce
½ teaspoon sugar
vegetable oil, extra, for deep frying

---

1 Separate wrappers. Cut each into 4 squares and cover with a cloth until needed.
2 Squeeze water from mushrooms, trim away stems, then shred finely. Cut chicken into small shreds.
3 Heat oil in a frying pan and cook chicken, mushrooms, spring onions, bamboo shoots and capsicum until the chicken turns white. Add the bean sprouts and cook briefly. Stir in soy sauce and sugar. Cool.
4 Place a spoonful of the filling on a wrapper and fold one point over it. Fold in the two side points, then roll up towards the last point, forming a log shape. Dip the end in water to stick down.
5 Deep-fry in moderately hot oil until pastry is golden. Drain and serve at once with plum sauce.

Add the sugar to the cooked chicken mixture and mix well.

Place a tablespoonful of the mixture on the wrapper.

Fold one point over the filling and fold in the sides.

Deep-fry the spring rolls in batches until lightly golden.

Prawn Toast

Serve with drinks or to start a Chinese meal.

Preparation time:
35 minutes
Cooking time:
15 minutes
Makes 36

1 spring onion (white part only)	*2–3 tablespoons cold water*
60 g water chestnut or bamboo shoots	*9 slices white bread*
200 g green prawn meat (about 450 g green prawns)	*3/4 cup white sesame seeds*
1 egg	*vegetable oil for deep frying*

1 In a food processor chop the spring onion and water chestnut or bamboo shoots. Add the prawn meat, egg and water. Grind to a smooth, light paste.

2 Spread prawn mixture evenly over each bread slice. Remove crusts and cut each slice into four triangles.

3 Dip into sesame seeds to coat evenly.

4 Deep-fry in moderately hot oil, filling side downwards until light golden. Turn and fry the bread side briefly, then remove and drain.

5 Serve hot with a sweet and sour or plum sauce.

Process prawn mixture until it is quite smooth.

Spread prawn mixture evenly over bread. Remove crusts.

Dip each triangle into sesame seeds to coat evenly.

Deep-fry in moderately hot oil until lightly golden.

Fried Dim Sims

Serve fried or steamed.

1 pack won ton
wrappers
600 g finely minced
pork
100 g bamboo shoots,
finely chopped
1 spring onion, finely
chopped
2 tablespoons finely
chopped fresh
coriander
2 tablespoons light
soy sauce
vegetable oil for deep
frying

Preparation time:
25 minutes
Cooking time:
15 minutes
Makes 20–24

1 Cover wrappers with a cloth until needed.
2 In a food processor grind pork until smooth. Transfer to a bowl. Add bamboo shoots, onion, coriander and sauce; work to smooth paste using hands.
3 To form the dumplings place a rounded tablespoon of the filling in the centre of a wrapper and press the edges of the wrapper up around the filling to almost enclose it. Squeeze gently so the wrapper adheres to the filling with the top of the filling partially exposed and the edges of the wrapper almost meeting on top. Tap the base of each Dim Sim on the table to flatten.

4 Heat deep oil to moderately hot and fry the Dim Sims, several at a time, until the pastry is golden brown, about 2 minutes. Remove and drain on absorbent paper.
5 Serve the Dim Sims hot with small dishes of soy sauce for dipping.

HINTS
☐ If preferred, instead of frying, steam the dumplings for about 6 minutes.
☐ This recipe also makes about 48 won tons. Use less filling and moisten the edges of the wrapper, fold into a triangle, pinch the edges together, then bring the two outer points together. Deep-fry or steam as above, allowing less cooking time than for dim sims.

Add finely chopped bamboo shoots, spring onion and coriander to pork mince.

Knead pork mixture to a smooth paste using hands.

Place a tablespoonful of filling in the centre of won ton wrapper.

Press edges of wrapper up and around filling to enclose them.

Crisp Quails with Pepper-Salt Dip

6 quails, halved
2 tablespoons dark soy sauce
1 teaspoon finely grated ginger
1 tablespoon dry sherry
vegetable oil for deep frying (optional)
2 tablespoons fine table salt
1 teaspoon Chinese peppercorns

Preparation time:
  15 minutes + 4 hours marinating
Cooking time:
  25 minutes
Serves 6–12

1 Place quails in a dish and brush evenly with the combined soy sauce, ginger and sherry. Cover with plastic wrap and leave to marinate in a cool place or in the refrigerator for 4 hours.
2 Drain quails and pat dry with kitchen paper. Bake in a hot oven for about 25 minutes or deep-fry in moderately hot oil until golden brown and cooked through, about 5 minutes. Remove and drain.
3 Heat salt in a dry wok for 3 minutes. Transfer to a mortar and pestle and grind with the peppercorns. Serve in a small dish.
4 Arrange quails on shredded lettuce and serve with the dip.

Brush quails with combined soy sauce, ginger and sherry.

Drain quails and wipe dry with absorbent kitchen paper.

Roast quails in a hot oven for about 25 minutes. Drain.

Grind salt and peppercorns using a processor or mortar and pestle.

Sweet Corn and Crabmeat Soup

Preparation time:
20 minutes
Cooking time:
10 minutes
Serves 4–6

---

2 cups frozen or
    canned sweet corn
    kernels
100 g crabmeat
1 spring onion, finely
    chopped
3¹/₂ cups water
2 teaspoons chicken
    stock powder

3 tablespoons
    cornflour
1¹/₂ tablespoons light
    soy sauce
2 tablespoons
    chopped spring
    onion greens to
    garnish

---

1 Chop the corn in a food processor until partially ground.

2 Mix corn, crabmeat and white parts of the spring onion in a saucepan, add water, stock powder and cornflour. Bring to the boil and simmer, stirring, until thickened.

3 Season with soy sauce. Pour into soup bowls and garnish with the spring onion greens.

> HINT
> This soup is equally delicious if it is made from 120 g finely chopped skinless chicken instead of the crabmeat.

Use a processor to partially grind sweet corn kernels.

Add water to the corn, crabmeat and spring onions.

Add stock powder and cornflour to soup mixture. Bring to the boil.

Season hot Sweet Corn Soup with soy sauce. Serve immediately.

Melon and Shredded Ham Soup

Preparation time:
   10 minutes
Cooking time:
   8 minutes
Serves 6

---

*1 x 600 g piece
   Chinese winter
   melon or use
   cucumbers
100 g ham
5 cups chicken stock
1 tablespoon finely
   sliced ginger
2 tablespoons finely
   sliced spring onion
1½ tablespoons light
   soy sauce*

---

to the boil. Reduce heat to simmering and add the melon, ginger, spring onion and soy sauce. Simmer 2 minutes until melon is tender. Add ham to soup, simmer 1 minute until warmed through.
3 Serve immediately.

1 Peel the melon. Cut into thin slices and then into 4 cm cubes. Slice the ham into long thin strips.
2 Place stock in a medium pan and bring

HINT
Steamed slices of winter melon can be served as a vegetable. Dress with a little cooked crabmeat moistened with chicken stock.

Peel winter melon and cut into thin slices, then into pieces.

Slice the ham into thin strips, each about 5 cm long.

Add shredded spring onion and ginger to soup mixture.

Add the ham strips to the simmering soup mixture.

13

Spicy Szechuan Soup

A spicy soup that's hearty and nourishing.

Preparation time:
35 minutes
Cooking time:
15 minutes
Serves 6

200 g firm bean curd	1–2 hot red chillies, seeded and finely shredded
60 g pork or calf's liver, very thinly sliced	2 tablespoons vegetable oil
100 g lean pork or chicken meat, very thinly sliced	60 g sliced bamboo shoots
4 dried Chinese black mushrooms, soaked	5 cups water
1 spring onion, chopped	2 teaspoons chicken stock powder
2 cloves garlic, chopped	2 tablespoons dark soy sauce
1 tablespoon finely shredded ginger	1 tablespoon Chinese black vinegar
1 small carrot, finely shredded	2 tablespoons chopped fresh coriander
2 sticks celery, thinly sliced	1/2 teaspoon cracked black pepper
	3 eggs, lightly beaten

1 Cut the bean curd into thin slices, then into narrow shreds. Cut the liver and meat slices into similar shreds.

2 Remove mushroom stems and shred the caps finely. Cook the mushrooms, spring onion, garlic, ginger, carrot, celery and chilli in the oil for 2 minutes. Add the pork or chicken and the bamboo shoots and cook briefly.

3 Add the water, chicken stock powder and soy sauce and bring to the boil. Simmer for 4 minutes.

4 Add the bean curd and liver, and the vinegar, coriander and pepper and heat through briefly. Then slowly pour in the beaten egg, stirring until the egg forms thin strands.

5 Serve the soup hot.

HINT
The Szechuan style of cooking is renowned for its use of fiery flavourings, mostly red chillies. This soup should have a sharp, tart taste — in fact the five flavours of traditional Szechuan foods — sweet, sour, salty, pungent and bitter — all appear in this nourishing soup. If you prefer a less sharp taste, you can reduce the amount of chilli and pepper.

Cut beancurd, liver and chicken or pork into thin shreds.

Add chicken stock powder to the simmering soup mixture.

Next add the beancurd and liver to the soup mixture.

Slowly pour in beaten egg and stir to form thin strands.

SEAFOOD

Seafood is a speciality of the eastern coastal region of China. The short, sharp stir-fry method of cooking suits shellfish and firm-fleshed fish. Spring onions and ginger flavour seafood dishes.

Stir-Fried Prawns with Leeks

Preparation time:
12 minutes
Cooking time:
4–5 minutes
Serves 6

---

800 g green king
    prawns in the shell
2 young leeks
1 fresh red chilli
1 x 3-cm piece ginger
3 tablespoons
    vegetable oil
2 teaspoons light soy
    sauce

1 tablespoon
    Japanese mirin or
    ginger wine
1/3 cup water
1/2 teaspoon chicken
    stock powder
1 teaspoon cornflour

---

1 Peel the prawns, leaving the last section of the shell and the tail intact. Slit open along the centre back and remove the vein.

2 Use only the white part of the leeks. Rinse well and cut first into 4-cm lengths and then lengthways into fine shreds. Slit open the chilli, remove and discard seeds and cut flesh into fine shreds. Peel the ginger and cut it into fine shreds.

3 Heat oil in a wok and stir-fry the leeks, chilli and ginger over high heat for 40 seconds. Push to one side of the wok, add the prawns and stir-fry for about 2 minutes until just cooked through.

4 Add the soy sauce and mirin or ginger wine to the wok. Mix water, chicken stock powder and cornflour and pour in. Cook on high heat, stirring until thickened.

Cut leek into thin shreds. Cut ginger and chilli into shreds.

Push leeks to one side of wok. Add prawns and stir-fry for 2 minutes.

Add the soy sauce to the prawns and leeks and mix well.

After adding cornflour mixture to prawns, stir until thickened.

Prawns in Satay Sauce

Preparation time:
    20 minutes
Cooking time:
    3 minutes
Serves 4

12 green king prawns
1 medium-sized onion
2 tablespoons vegetable oil
$^1/_4$ cup bottled satay sauce

1 Peel the prawns, leaving the last section of the shell and the tail intact. Cut deeply down the centre back, remove the dark vein, and flatten prawns slightly.

2 Peel the onion, trim away the root section and cut into curved slices by cutting from top to base. Separate the pieces.

3 Heat oil in a wok and stir-fry the onion until it begins to soften. Add the prawns and stir-fry until they are lightly cooked, about 1½ minutes. Add the satay sauce and mix well. Serve immediately with boiled rice and Chinese greens.

HINT

This recipe is also very good when made with scallops. Wash the scallops well to get rid of sand. Discard the membrane round the white meat. The red roe can be eaten, however.

Cut curved slices of onion by cutting from top to the base.

Add peeled and deveined prawns to stir-fried onions.

Stir-fry prawns and onions over a high heat until prawns are pink.

Add a ¼ cup of bottled satay sauce to prawns, mix well.

Stuffed Scallops with Snow Peas

12 large fresh scallops
1 spring onion
100 g shelled prawns
2 teaspoons dry sherry or rice wine
1 tablespoon light soy sauce
½ cup cornflour
2 cups vegetable oil
1 teaspoon finely shredded ginger
100 g fresh snow peas
⅔ cup water
½ teaspoon chicken stock powder

1 Dry the scallops with kitchen paper and set aside.

Preparation time:
   30 minutes
Cooking time:
   7 minutes
Serves 4

2 Chop the white part of the spring onion in a food processor and then add the prawns and half the sherry and half the soy sauce. Add 2 teaspoons cornflour.
3 Cover the top of each scallop generously with the prawn mixture and roll in cornflour.
4 Heat the oil and fry the scallops until the surface is lightly golden and then remove to a serving plate.
5 Pour off the oil and wipe out the pan. Return 2 tablespoons

of the oil to the pan and stir-fry the snow peas briefly with the chopped spring onion greens and ginger. Add water mixed with chicken stock powder, 2 teaspoons cornflour and the remaining sherry and soy sauce. Stir until thickened.
6 Pour the snow peas and sauce over the scallops and serve at once.

HINTS
☐ A more economical dish can be made either by using fish instead of prawns for the stuffing, or by using half the number of scallops and cutting them in halves horizontally.
☐ Never overcook stir-fried dishes. Vegetables should retain their crispness.

Use a teaspoon to cover the top of each scallop with prawn mixture.

Roll each stuffed scallop to cover evenly with cornflour.

Deep-fry the stuffed scallops in batches until golden. Drain.

Stir in combined water, stock powder, cornflour, sherry and soy sauce.

Steamed Whole Fish

Use fresh fish.

Preparation time:
35 minutes
Cooking time:
12 minutes
Serves 4–6

1 kg whole snapper or other large white fish	*¼ red capsicum or fresh red chilli*
2 dried Chinese black mushrooms, soaked	*1 x 3-cm piece ginger*
1 small carrot	*1 tablespoon vegetable oil*
1 large spring onion	*1½ tablespoons light soy sauce*

1 Scale the fish, rinse and wipe dry. Make several deep cuts diagonally across both sides.

2 Drain mushrooms, squeeze out water and remove stems. Cut all the vegetables and the ginger into fine matchstick pieces.

3 Place the fish on a plate and scatter the vegetables and ginger over it. Add oil and soy sauce.

4 Set the plate on a rack in a steamer over gently simmering water. Cover tightly and steam for about 12 minutes, or until the fish is cooked through. (Test after 9–10 minutes.)

Make several deep cuts diagonally across both sides of fish.

Slice carrot, spring onion, capsicum, mushrooms and ginger in thin shreds.

Place fish on a large plate. Scatter vegetables over fish.

Pour oil and soy sauce over fish. Steam for about 12 minutes.

Crab in Black Bean Sauce

Preparation time:
40 minutes
Cooking time:
10 minutes
Serves 4

4 crabs	1 teaspoon finely
1 medium onion	chopped garlic
1/2 red capsicum	1 teaspoon finely
1/2 green capsicum	chopped ginger
2 spring onions	1 teaspoon sugar
1/2 cup oil	1 tablespoon light soy
3 teaspoons finely	sauce
chopped salted	1/3 cup water
black beans	2 teaspoons cornflour

1 Remove flap from the belly of each crab.
2 Prise off top shell, discard soft grey entails. Wash crabs and cut in half. Remove claws.

3 Cut vegetables into strips. Heat oil in wok. Cook crab pieces in oil for 3 minutes, drain. Strain oil, return 2 tablespoons oil to wok.
4 Stir-fry black beans, garlic and ginger for 30 seconds. Add sugar and vegetables. Stir-fry for 2 minutes. Add crab. Add soy sauce and water mixed with cornflour. Cook until sauce boils and thickens. Remove from heat and serve immediately.

Lift flap from underbelly of each crab and break off.

Prise off top shell and remove soft grey entails. Wash crabs.

Add onion, capsicum, and spring onion to wok. Stir-fry 2 minutes.

Add crab and combined soy sauce, water and cornflour. Stir until thickened.

Fish, Asparagus and Mushroom Parcels

Preparation time:
    35 minutes
Cooking time:
    10 minutes
Serves 4

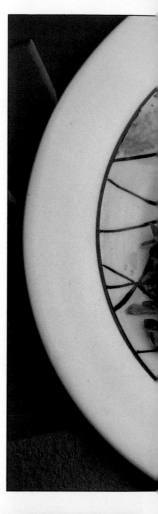

*500 g white fish
    fillets
2 spring onions
1 tablespoon oil
1 tablespoon finely
    shredded ginger
2 tablespoons flaked
    almonds
1 x 425 g can straw
    mushrooms,
    drained
½ cup chicken stock
1 teaspoon cornflour
¼ cup oyster sauce
200 g asparagus, cut
    diagonally into
    3 cm pieces*

1 Place each fish fillet on a piece of foil large enough to enclose the fillet.

2 Cut spring onions in halves lengthways and then into 4 cm pieces.

3 Heat oil in wok, add spring onions, ginger, almonds and mushrooms. Stir-fry for 30 seconds.

4 Stir in combined stock, cornflour and oyster sauce. Stir over medium heat till thickened. Remove from heat, stir in asparagus. Cool.

5 Spoon mixture evenly over fillets and enclose with foil. Place fish parcels in steamer. Steam, covered, for 10 minutes or until fish is tender.

Stir-fry spring onions, ginger, almonds and mushrooms for 30 seconds.

Add the combined stock, cornflour and oyster sauce.

Spoon asparagus mushroom mixture evenly over fish parcels.

Enclose each fish parcel and place parcels in a single layer in steamer.

Sizzling Seafood on Crisp Rice Noodles

Preparation time:
  40 minutes
Cooking time:
  10 minutes
Serves 4–6

---

6 medium-sized
  green prawns
200 g cod or other
  white fish
4 calamari tubes
6 scallops
2 cups vegetable oil
150 g rice vermicelli
1 medium onion,
  sliced from top to
  base
1 stalk celery, sliced
  diagonally

200 g snow peas,
  trimmed
12 paper-thin slices
  ginger
¼ cup tomato sauce
1 teaspoon chicken
  stock powder
2 teaspoons sugar
1 teaspoon chilli
  sauce
1 tablespoon
  cornflour
1½ cups water

---

1 Peel the prawns and devein. Cut fish into bite-sized cubes, slice the calamari and halve the scallops.
2 Heat the oil and fry the vermicelli in small batches until it expands and turns white. Remove quickly to avoid overcooking. Spread on a serving platter.
3 Pour off all but 3 tablespoons of the oil and stir-fry the vegetables for about 2 minutes. Remove or push to the side of the pan and stir-fry the seafood until cooked. Mix with the vegetables and spread evenly over the vermicelli.
4 Place tomato sauce, stock powder, sugar and chilli sauce in pan. Mix well. Combine cornflour with water and mix until smooth. Add cornflour to pan, stirring constantly over medium heat until the sauce mixture boils and thickens. Pour over the vermicelli and seafood and serve immediately.

Slice calamari into rings, peel and devein prawns, cut fish into cubes.

Fry vermicelli in small batches until it expands and turns white.

Stir-fry snow peas, celery, ginger and onion in wok for about 2¹/₂ minutes.

Stir the combined water and cornflour into the sauce.

Crabmeat Omelette

6 eggs
2 teaspoons light soy
    sauce
pinch each of sugar
    and white pepper
2 small spring
    onions, chopped
2 tablespoons
    vegetable oil
150 g flaked
    crabmeat
1–1¹/₂ tablespoons
    oyster sauce

Preparation time:
    15 minutes
Cooking time:
    5–6 minutes
Serves 2–4

1 Beat the eggs with soy sauce, sugar and pepper and 2 tablespoons water.

2 Heat a wok or omelette pan and cook white parts of the spring onions in the oil for 30 seconds. Add crabmeat and cook briefly, and then pour in the egg. Cook until set and lightly coloured underneath, cut into 4 pieces, turn and cook the other side.

3 Transfer to a warmed plate, drizzle over the oyster sauce and garnish with the chopped spring onion greens.

HINT
You can also make this omelette with stir-fried peeled prawns, diced chicken or a combination of diced meats and vegetables.

Combine eggs, soy sauce, sugar, pepper and water, whisk well.

Cook spring onions for about 30 seconds, add crabmeat, cook briefly.

Pour egg mixture into pan, cook until underside is lightly coloured.

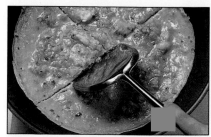

Use a spatula to cut omelette into four, turn and cook other side.

MEAT & CHICKEN

Meat and chicken dishes are best prepared completely before beginning to cook. Sauces and seasonings are added to flavour and tenderise the meats, while vegetables are cut into even sized pieces for stir-frying.

Sweet and Sour Pork

One of the most favoured Chinese dishes.

Preparation time:
20 minutes + 20 minutes marinating
Cooking time:
12 minutes
Serves 4–6

> 700 g pork belly or spare ribs
> 1 tablespoon light soy sauce
> 1 tablespoon dry sherry
> 1/2 medium cucumber
> 2 tablespoons Chinese sweet mixed pickles
> 1 cup cornflour
> 5 cups vegetable oil
> 1/4 green capsicum, shredded
> 1/4 red capsicum, shredded
> 1 medium onion, sliced from top to base
> 1/2 cup white vinegar
> 1 cup water
> 1/4 cup tomato sauce
> 1/3 cup sugar
> 1 teaspoon powdered chicken stock
> 1 tablespoon cornflour, extra

1 Thickly slice the pork, then cut into 1-cm strips crossways so that each piece consists of layers of pork and fat. Remove any small bones from spare ribs. Brush with sherry and soy; set aside 20 minutes.

2 Peel the cucumber, cut in half and scoop out the seeds, then cut into thin slices. Finely chop the pickles or cut into fine shreds.

3 Coat the pork thickly with cornflour and shake off the excess. Fry in several batches in the oil until lightly golden, about 2 minutes. Remove and spread on a rack to drain and cool.

4 Stir-fry the capsicum and onion in 3 tablespoons of oil taken from the frying pan. (Reserve the remaining hot oil for a second fry of the pork.) Add the cucumber and pickles and fry briefly, then add the vinegar, water, tomato sauce, sugar, chicken stock and cornflour. Stir until the cornflour is dissolved. Bring to the boil and simmer, stirring, until thickened.

5 Reheat the oil and fry the pork a second time until golden and crisp, about 2 minutes. Pour on the sauce and serve hot with white steamed rice.

Slice pork into 1 cm thick slices. Remove any small bones.

Peel, seed and thinly slice cucumber. Finely chop pickles.

Deep-fry pork in several batches until lightly golden.

Add combined vinegar, water, tomato sauce, sugar, stock and cornflour to wok.

Spare Ribs in Black Bean Sauce

Preparation time:
15 minutes
Cooking time:
1 hour 40 minutes
Serves 6–8

1 kg meaty spare ribs
2 tablespoons salted black beans, chopped
4–6 cloves garlic, finely chopped
2 tablespoons chopped ginger
1 fresh red chilli, finely chopped
¼ cup light soy sauce
1 tablespoon dark soy sauce
3 tablespoons brown sugar
1½ cups water
2 tablespoons vegetable oil
1 large onion, chopped
1 green capsicum, chopped

1 Cut ribs into 4-cm pieces; place in ovenproof dish. Scatter on black beans, garlic, ginger and chilli; add soy sauces, sugar and water.

2 Cover the dish and bake in preheated moderate oven (180°C) or place in a steamer and cook over gently simmering water for 1½ hours.

3 Heat oil in wok and stir-fry onion and capsicum until softened. Add pork ribs and juices and cook 5-6 minutes. Serve hot with rice.

Cut ribs into 4-cm pieces. Place in dish and sprinkle with black beans.

Pour combined soy, sugar and water over spare ribs.

Heat oil in wok. Stir-fry onion and
capsicum for about 2 minutes.

Add cooked pork ribs and juices to wok.
Stir-fry 5–6 minutes.

Shredded Pork and Vegetables on Noodles

Fresh egg noodles are best.

300 g lean pork	6 small cauliflower
1 tablespoon dark	florets
soy sauce	1/4 red capsicum, cut
1 tablespoon sweet	into squares
sherry	1 small onion, sliced
1 tablespoon	from top to bottom
cornflour	1/4 cup vegetable oil
1 celery stick	1 cup chicken stock
1/2 medium carrot	1 1/2 teaspoons
6 small broccoli	cornflour, extra
florets	4 bundles egg noodles

Preparation time:
  30 minutes + 30
    minutes marinating
Cooking time:
  20 minutes
Serves 4–6

1 Cut the pork into fine shreds and place in a dish with the soy sauce, sherry and cornflour. Mix well and leave for 30 minutes.
2 Cut the celery and carrot into matchstick pieces. Cook all the vegetables in one-third of the oil for about 2 minutes. Remove and keep warm. Add the meat and marinade and another one-third of the oil. Stir-fry until it changes colour; then add the stock mixed with cornflour. Cook, stirring until the sauce thickens. Then return the vegetables. Mix well.
3 Drop noodles into boiling water to soften. Disentangle the bundles, remove and drain.
4 Cook the noodles in the remaining oil until well coated with the oil, transfer to a serving plate and pour on the meat and vegetables. Serve at once.

Cut the broccoli and cauliflower into small florets.

Stir-fry pork until it changes colour. Combine stock and cornflour.

Briefly cook noodles in boiling water until soft. Drain well.

Stir-fry drained noodles in wok until well coated with oil and hot.

Sizzling Mongolian Lamb

🥢 🥢

400 g lean boneless
  lamb
1 teaspoon finely
  chopped garlic
2 teaspoons grated
  ginger
1 tablespoon dark
  soy sauce
1 tablespoon dry
  sherry
1 tablespoon sesame
  oil
2 teaspoons cornflour
1 large onion
2 tablespoons
  vegetable oil
2 teaspoons sesame
  seeds (optional)

Preparation time:
  20 minutes + 2
  hours marinating
Cooking time:
  5–6 minutes
Serves 4

1 Cut the lamb into paper thin slices and then into short strips. Place in a dish and add the garlic, ginger, soy sauce, sherry, sesame oil and cornflour. Mix well and leave to marinate for 2 hours.

2 Cut the onion into curved slices by cutting from top to base. Separate the pieces.

3 Heat oil in a wok. Stir-fry onions briefly. Remove. Stir-fry meat for about 1–2 minutes or until just cooked. Return onions to wok.

4 Serve, sprinkled with sesame seeds. If preferred, serve meat spooned over onions.

Cut lamb into paper-thin slices, and then into short strips.

Add garlic, ginger, soy, sherry, sesame oil and cornflour to lamb.

Heat oil in wok, add sliced onion and stir-fry for about 1 minute.

Stir-fry lamb until just cooked. Return onion to wok and mix well.

Stir-Fried Beef with Broccoli

400 g rump steak
1 tablespoon
    cornflour
2 tablespoons light
    soy sauce
1 tablespoon dry
    sherry
1 teaspoon sugar
150 g broccoli
3 tablespoons oil
2 spring onions
    (white parts only),
    sliced
1/2 cup chicken or
    beef stock
1 1/4 tablespoons
    oyster sauce
    (optional)

Preparation time:
    15 minutes + 30
        minutes marinating
Cooking time:
    3–4 minutes
Serves 4

1 Slice the beef very thinly. Put in a dish with the cornflour, soy sauce, sherry and sugar. Mix well and leave for 30 minutes.
2 Divide the broccoli into small florets and stir-fry in the oil for about 1 minute. Add the spring onions and fry briefly. Push to one side of the pan and add the beef and marinade. Stir-fry on high heat until the meat changes colour, about 2 minutes.
3 Add the stock and cook on high heat, stirring, for about 1 minute. Stir in the oyster sauce, if used.
4 Serve with white rice.

Thinly slice beef and combine with cornflour, soy, sherry and sugar.

Stir-fry broccoli about 1 minute. Add spring onions.

Push broccoli to one side. Add beef and marinade and stir-fry 2 minutes.

Add stock to wok and cook, stirring for about 1 minute.

Shredded Chicken and Bean Sprouts

Preparation time:
  15 minutes + 20
    minutes marinating
Cooking time:
  2–3 minutes
Serves 4

---

300 g skinless
  chicken breast
1 tablespoon light
  soy sauce
1 teaspoon sugar
1 teaspoon cornflour
3 spring onions
  (white parts only),
  shredded
3 tablespoons
  vegetable oil
1 tablespoon dry
  sherry
125 g fresh bean
  sprouts
¹/₂ cup chicken stock
1 teaspoon cornflour

---

1 Slice, then finely shred the chicken and marinate with soy sauce, sugar and cornflour for 20 minutes. (See Note).

2 Stir-fry the spring onions in the oil for 30 seconds, push to one side of the pan and stir-fry the chicken. Add the sherry.

3 Add bean sprouts and stir-fry briefly. Mix chicken stock and cornflour, stir into the dish and cook, stirring, until thickened.

Note. Marination is essential when cooking by the fast stir-fry method, to allow seasonings to penetrate.

Stir soy sauce mixture into chicken.
Marinate for 20 minutes.

Stir-fry the spring onions in oil for 30 seconds.

Add the sherry to the chicken mixture and mix well.

Pour combined chicken stock and cornflour into wok. Stir until thickened.

Honey Chicken

Preparation time:
   10 minutes
Cooking time:
   10 minutes
Serves 4–6

---

*500 g skinless
   chicken breast
1 cup cornflour
½ teaspoon baking
   powder
2 egg whites
cold water
extra cornflour for
   dusting chicken
¾ cup clear
   honey
1½ teaspoons sweet
   chilli sauce
spring onion for
   garnish*

pieces with cornflour, then dip into the batter. Deep-fry for about 1 minute until crisp on the surface and cooked through.

3 In another pan melt the honey with chilli sauce. Pour over the chicken and serve immediately. Garnish with spring onion.

1 Cut the chicken into bite-sized pieces.

2 Make a creamy batter of the cornflour, baking powder, beaten egg whites and cold water. Dust chicken

HINT

Try serving this dish on a bed of crisply fried rice noodles. Drop handfuls of the noodles into hot oil, fry just long enough for them to expand and turn white, then remove.

Make a batter of the cornflour, baking powder, beaten egg whites and water.

Dust the chicken pieces evenly with the extra cornflour.

Deep-fry chicken pieces in moderately hot oil until golden.

To make spring onion curls for garnish, cut thin shreds and cool in iced water.

Stir-Fried Chicken with Peanuts and Chilli

Preparation time:
15 minutes + 30 minutes marinating
Cooking time:
8 minutes
Serves 4–6

---

400 g boneless chicken breast with skin
1 teaspoon finely grated ginger
1 tablespoon dry sherry
1 tablespoon light soy sauce
1 fresh or dried red chilli, sliced
1/2 cup raw peanuts, skinned
1/2 cup vegetable oil
1 medium onion, sliced from top to base
1 small red capsicum, cut into diamonds
1 small green capsicum, cut into diamonds
1 cup bamboo shoots
1/2 cup chicken stock
1 teaspoon chilli sauce (optional)
2 teaspoons cornflour

---

1 Cut the chicken into 2-cm cubes and place in a dish with the ginger, sherry and soy sauce. Mix well and marinate for 30 minutes.

2 Fry the chilli and peanuts in hot oil for about 1 minute and remove. Pour off half the oil. Stir-fry the onion, capsicum and bamboo shoots for 1 minute, then remove or push to the side of the pan and stir-fry the chicken for about 2 minutes or until just cooked through.

3 Add the combined chicken stock, sauce and cornflour. Bring to the boil over high heat, stirring until thickened.

4 Return capsicum mixture and stir in chilli and peanuts. Heat through briefly.

HINT
Make this dish also with large prawns, diced pork, or cubes of bean curd previously fried in oil to crisp the surface.

Marinate chicken in ginger, sherry and soy sauce. Mix well.

Stir-fry the peanuts in hot oil for about 1 minute.

Push the onion mixture to the edge of the pan. Add chicken.

Stir in combined stock, sauce and cornflour. Bring to boil, stir until thickened.

VEGETABLES

Vegetables are used in Chinese dishes to add colour, texture and fragrance. Red and green capsicum, onion and Chinese leafy greens like choy sum, bok choy and Chinese broccoli are the most popular.

Cantonese Fried Rice

2¹/₂ cups short-grain white rice
¹/₂ cup green peas
¹/₂ cup sweet corn kernels
¹/₂ cup vegetable oil
3 rashers bacon, cut in 1 cm wide strips
¹/₂ small red capsicum, diced
2 spring onions, chopped
2 eggs, lightly beaten
100 g small peeled cooked prawns
2 tablespoons light soy sauce

Preparation time:
  15 minutes
Cooking time:
  30 minutes
Serves 4–6

1 Place rice and 3 cups cold water in a heavy saucepan, cover and bring to the boil. Reduce heat to very lowest setting and cook for about 18 minutes until the rice has absorbed the liquid and each grain is plump and separate.

2 Boil the peas and corn in water until just tender; drain.

3 Heat half the oil in a wok and stir-fry the bacon until cooked. Add the capsicum and spring onions, stir-fry for 1 minute and then remove. Pour in the beaten egg and turn the pan to spread the egg widely over the bottom. Cook until firm underneath, then break up with a spatula and remove. Wipe out the pan.

4 Heat the remaining oil and toss the rice over high heat for 2 minutes. Add the cooked ingredients and prawns and sprinkle on the soy sauce. Continue tossing over high heat for a few minutes. Serve hot.

Stir-fry bacon until just cooked. Add capsicum and spring onions.

Break up cooked egg with a spatula. Remove egg and wipe wok.

Add the cooked ingredients to the rice.
Stir well to mix and heat.

Add soy sauce and stir well to mix and
heat through. Serve immediately.

Stir-Fried Vegetable Assortment

Preparation time:
   10 minutes
Cooking time:
   5 minutes
Serves 4–6

---

1 medium onion
2 stalks celery,
   diagonally sliced
1 medium carrot,
   sliced
1 small zucchini,
   sliced
8 green beans, sliced
6 small broccoli
   florets
6 small cauliflower
   florets

60 g sliced bamboo
   shoots
12 snow peas
12 straw mushrooms
12 baby corn cobs
3 tablespoons
   vegetable oil
100 g fresh bean
   sprouts
³⁄₄ cup chicken stock
1 tablespoon light soy
   sauce
3 teaspoons cornflour

---

1 Peel the onion and cut in halves. Cut off the base section by slicing away diagonally to release the layers. Slice the onion by cutting from the top to base to give slightly curved slices.

2 Slice the celery Chinese style by cutting diagonally across the stalks.

3 Heat oil in a wok and stir-fry the vegetables together for about 5 minutes until cooked but still crisp.

4 Mix chicken stock, soy sauce and cornflour together and pour into the pan. Cook on high heat, stirring, until the sauce thickens and clears. Serve at once.

HINT
Other vegetables such as Chinese greens like bok choy, Chinese broccoli and choy sum can be used in this dish. All are available from Chinese grocers, particularly in areas with a sizeable Chinese population. Add finely shredded ginger and a good dash of sherry for extra flavour.

Slice the celery diagonally across the stalks.

Heat oil in wok. Add vegetables, stir-frying until cooked but still crisp.

Add combined chicken stock and soy sauce to cornflour; mix well.

Pour chicken stock mixture into wok, stirring until sauce thickens.

Chinese Vegetables with Mushrooms and Oyster Sauce

Preparation time:
  20 minutes
Cooking time:
  8 minutes
Serves 4

---

*1 bunch Chinese
  green vegetables
  (bok choy, choy
  sum, gai larn)*
*8 dried Chinese
  black mushrooms,
  soaked*
*2 tablespoons
  vegetable oil*
*2 tablespoons oyster
  sauce*

---

1 Thoroughly wash vegetables and drain well. Cut off thick stalks from greens and cut the leaves and stalks into strips.
2 Trim stems from mushrooms, squeeze water from caps. Simmer in lightly salted water for 5 minutes then drain.
3 Plunge the vegetable stems into boiling water to cook for 1–2 minutes. Remove, then briefly blanch the leafy parts and drain well.
4 Toss vegetables and mushrooms in oil over moderate heat till well coated. Serve dressed with oyster sauce.

HINT
Canned straw mushrooms or champignons can replace the black mushrooms.

Cut off thick stalks from greens. Cut stalks into thin strips.

Simmer Chinese dried mushrooms until tender.

Plunge the leafy parts of the greens into boiling water.

Stir-fry stalks, leafy greens and mushrooms in wok for about 1 minute.

Spicy Hot Bean Curd with Minced Beef

Preparation time:
20 minutes
Cooking time:
10 minutes
Serves 4–6

300 g topside mince
1 medium-sized
  onion, chopped
2 tablespoons
  vegetable oil
1¹/₂ teaspoons finely
  chopped garlic
2 teaspoons finely
  chopped ginger
¹/₂–1 tablespoon
  Chinese hot bean
  paste

1–2 teaspoons sugar
1 tablespoon dark soy
  sauce
500 g soft bean curd,
  cubed
³/₄ cup chicken stock
1 tablespoon
  cornflour
large lettuce leaves for
  serving

1 Stir-fry the minced beef and onion in the oil for 4 minutes.
2 Add the garlic and ginger and fry briefly. Then add the bean paste, sugar and soy sauce and cook for about 1¹/₂ minutes, stirring frequently.
3 Add the bean curd and the combined stock and cornflour and cook gently, stirring, until the sauce thickens. Serve in lettuce cups.

Stir-fry the minced beef and onion until well coloured, about 4 minutes.

Add garlic and ginger and stir-fry for about 1 minute.

Add the bean paste, sugar and soy sauce. Stir-fry for about 2 minutes.

Add the combined stock and cornflour. Stir gently until sauce thickens.

SWEETS

Desserts as we know them are generally not served as part of a Chinese meal. Sweet treats are served as a snack or for a special occasion.

Coconut Jelly

400 mL coconut
  cream
1 cup milk
2 cups water
½ cup sugar
1 x 12 g sachet
  agar-agar powder
½ cup desiccated
  coconut

Preparation time:
  15 minutes + 1
  hour setting time
Cooking time:
  5 minutes
Makes 24 squares
  (serves 8–12)

1 Pour the coconut cream, milk and water into a saucepan. Add sugar and agar-agar and mix well.
2 Bring to the boil and simmer, stirring, for 3 minutes. Stir in the desiccated coconut.
3 Pour into a wet sandwich tin and leave to cool and set. Cut into squares. Serve cold.

HINT
To replace the coconut cream, use 1½ cups of desiccated coconut mixed in a food processor or blender with the milk and water, adding an extra half cup of water.

Pour water into a pan with the coconut cream and milk.

Add combined sugar and agar-agar to pan and mix well.

Stir the desiccated coconut into the pan.

Pour into a wet tin. Leave to cool and set at room temperature.

Deep-Fried Ice-cream in Coconut

Use quality ice-cream.

> 2 L vanilla ice-cream
> 1 egg
> 1 cup flour
> 3/4 cup water
> 1 1/2 cups fine dry
> breadcrumbs
> 2 tablespoons
> desiccated coconut
> 5 cups deep-frying
> oil

Preparation time:
  20 minutes +
  several days freezing
Cooking time:
  20 seconds
Serves 6

1 Make 6 large scoops of ice-cream. Return to the freezer.
2 Make a thick batter of egg, flour and water. Coat ice-cream balls with the batter, then roll in the bread-crumbs and coconut to coat thickly. Return to the freezer to freeze for several days.
3 Heat the oil to moderately hot. Slide in one ice-cream ball at a time to cook for a few seconds until the surface is golden. Remove and serve at once with caramel topping or fresh fruit.

HINT
It is crucial that the ice-cream is solidly frozen and that the oil is sufficiently hot to seal and cook the surface coconut in just a few seconds.

Use an ice-cream scoop to make 6 large scoops of ice-cream.

Mix the egg, flour and water to make a thick batter.

Coat each ice-cream ball evenly with combined breadcrumbs and coconut.

Deep-fry ice-cream balls one at a time for a few seconds or until golden.

SAUCES

Here are two special sauces, ideal to serve as dipping sauces for any of the fried or steamed snacks in this book. They are both best served hot, and can be stored, covered in the refrigerator for up to a week.

Sweet and Sour Sauce

1 cup water
¹/₂ cup white vinegar
¹/₂ cup sugar
3 tablespoons tomato sauce or ¹/₃ teaspoon red food colouring
1 teaspoon chicken stock powder
1 tablespoon cornflour

Mix the ingredients in a small saucepan, bring to the boil and simmer until thickened.

Spicy Plum Sauce

1 x 400 g can plums
¹/₃ cup vinegar
1 tablespoon sugar
¹/₄ teaspoon Chinese five-spice
2 teaspoons cornflour

1 Pit the plums and place with liquid in a food processor and process to a purée.
2 Transfer to a saucepan, add the remaining ingredients and simmer, stirring, until thickened.

Preparation time for each recipe:
10 minutes
Cooking time:
5 minutes
Each recipe makes 1¹/₂ cups

HINT
Give added flavour to Sweet and Sour Sauce by adding one of the following: 2 tablespoons finely chopped pineapple, 2 teaspoons shredded ginger, 1 tablespoon finely chopped Chinese pickles, ¹/₂ teaspoon cracked black pepper. Add bottled chilli sauce to Spicy Plum Sauce for added zest, or try a little ground ginger or cinnamon.
Serve sauces with spring rolls, prawn toast or gow gees.

Sweet and Sour Sauce: Add water and sugar to vinegar in a small pan.

Stir in tomato sauce, stock and cornflour and bring to the boil.

Spicy Plum Sauce (left) and Sweet and Sour Sauce (right)

Spicy Plum Sauce: Remove stones from plums; process plums and juice to a purée.

Add combined vinegar, sugar, five-spice powder and cornflour.

61

GLOSSARY

Agar-Agar: A type of gelatine made from seaweed. It does not require refrigeration, and produces a firm jelly with an interesting crunchy texture.

Bamboo Shoots: Cream-coloured shoots of the bamboo plant used as a vegetable. Sold in cans, whole or sliced; can sometimes be bought fresh from Chinese vegetable markets. Store unused bamboo shoots in water for several days only, in the refrigerator.

Bean Curd: A soft ochre-coloured jelly-like ingredient made by gelling a mixture of ground and strained soya beans and water. Sold in little plastic tubs packed with water as 'soft' for adding to soups, meat and vegetable dishes; 'firm' for slicing to fry or to add to braised dishes; and 'compressed' which is even firmer and can be fried until well browned on the surface.

Bean Sprouts: Creamy yellow shoots sprouted from the green mung bean (and larger deeper yellow ones from soya beans). Soak briefly in iced water before use to make them crisp. Will keep for only a few days in the refrigerator.

Black Beans: Salted and fermented soya beans which are deep black and soft. They are chopped to use as a salty seasoning.

Chillies/Chilli Sauce: Fresh red chillies should be slit open and seeds removed before use. Wear rubber gloves to avoid skin irritation. Hot Chinese chilli sauce is sold in small bottles and should be kept in the refrigerator. Sweet chilli sauces are used as a dip and in some recipes.

Chinese Five-Spice: A fine spice powder made from five sweet spices — cassia, clove, fennel, star anise and Chinese peppercorns. Mixed with salt it is used as a dip for fried foods, and is added to some dishes.

Chinese Green Vegetables: Rather like overgrown cabbages with deep green leafy stems on long thin stalks. They are sold at Chinese vegetable markets and will keep in the refrigerator for several days. Cut stalks into 10-cm lengths and cook longer than leaves.

Chinese Peppercorns: Small red-brown dried berries which have a sweet fragrance and are only mildly peppery. Used whole to flavour stews and soups; ground peppercorns are mixed with salt as a dip or condiment.

Coriander: The leafy fronds of the seed spice coriander, it is more commonly known as Chinese parsley.

Corn, Baby Cobs: Sold in cans, and sometimes fresh, these miniature cobs with their pleasing crunchy texture and bland taste are a popular addition to stir-fried dishes.

Ginger: Fresh root ginger should be skinned and very thinly sliced, chopped or shredded. Dried ginger is not a substitute, but crystallised ginger can be used in emergencies.

Mushrooms, Black: These expensive dried mushrooms should be stored in a cool, dark, dry place to prevent them going mouldy. Soak for 20 minutes in hot water before use, trim off the hard stem and use caps whole or shredded. The water mushrooms have been soaked in can be added to sauces or soups.

Noodles: Egg noodles are sold in small tangled bundles. Soak or briefly boil to untangle before use. Fresh noodles need only brief cooking in boiling salted water.

Oyster Sauce: A thick brown salty sauce made by fermenting oysters. Always store in the refrigerator.

Rice Vermicelli: Very thin whitish strands of a hard type of pasta made from rice flour. They should be soaked in warm water to soften and require very little cooking. If they are to be fried, do not soak, but add directly to moderately hot oil and cook just long enough for them to treble in size and turn white and crisp.

Satay Sauce: Bottled satay sauce comprises ground roasted peanuts with spices. Store in the refrigerator.

Sesame Oil: A dark brown oil with a strong, nutty flavour made from sesame seeds. Used to add flavour to fried foods and in marinades.

Sherry/Rice Wine/ Ginger Wine: Dry sherry is a suitable substitute for rice wine. Ginger wine also gives a good flavour.

Soy Sauce, light and dark: Light soy sauce is used when a salty taste is required, dark soy when a dish requires a darker colour.

Spring Roll Wrappers: Thin parchment-like wrappers sold in packs of 12–20 pieces. Used to wrap fried foods, they turn very crisp when fried. Keep damp during use by covering with a slightly moistened cloth. Store unused wrappers, well wrapped in plastic, in the freezer.

Straw Mushrooms: Sold in cans, and sometimes fresh, they are small, deep grey ball-shaped mushrooms which in cross-section reveal the shape of another smaller mushroom inside. Once opened, they do not keep for more than a few days in the refrigerator.

Vegetable Oil: A mild vegetable oil is used for deep frying, but Chinese prefer a 'cooked' oil for stir-frying. The oil that has been used once or twice for deep-frying can be used as the main oil for stir-frying, as it has lost its 'raw' taste.

Vinegar, Chinese Black: Sold in Chinese food stores, it is a dark, mild-tasting vinegar. Substitute malt vinegar, rice vinegar or cider vinegar diluted with water.

Water Chestnuts: Small rounded crisp vegetables sold in cans and sometimes fresh. They have an agreeable crunchy texture and a bland, very slightly sweet taste. Store unused water chestnuts under water in a plastic container in the refrigerator for several days only.

Winter Melon: This gigantic melon looks like a water melon, but has bland tasting cream-green flesh.

Won Ton Wrappers: Small thin squares of pasta dough, made from egg yolks and flour. Sold in stacks of around 30, they can be stored in the refrigerator for several days.

INDEX